THE
ISAIAH
VISION

Natasha Swartzloff
November 1995

Raymond Fung

THE ISAIAH *VISION*

An Ecumenical
Strategy for
Congregational
Evangelism

Risk
BOOK SERIES

WCC Publications, Geneva

Second printing: July 1992
Third printing: April 1993

Cover design: Rob Lucas

ISBN 2-8254-1037-3

© 1992 WCC Publications, World Council of Churches,
150 route de Ferney, 1211 Geneva 2, Switzerland

Risk book series No. 52

Printed in Switzerland

Table of Contents

Introduction

There are many Christian organizations and missionary societies which engage in evangelism and the promotion of evangelism. There are crusades and rallies, specialized events and training programmes to facilitate the spread of the good news. But at the end of the day, it is the local congregation, in its life and ministry, that must address the task of witnessing to Jesus Christ before every person and in every neighbourhood, day in and day out, year in and year out.

That is why the WCC has this to say in its *Mission and Evangelism: An Ecumenical Affirmation:*

> It is at the heart of Christian mission to foster the multiplication of local congregations in every human community. The planting of the seed of the gospel will bring forward a people gathered around the word and sacraments and called to announce God's revealed purpose.
>
> Thanks to the faithful witness of disciples through the ages, churches have sprung up in practically every country. *This task of sowing the seed needs to be continued until there is, in every human community, a cell of the kingdom, a church confessing Jesus Christ and in his name serving his people.* The building up of the church in every place is essential to the gospel. The vicarious work of Christ demands the presence of a vicarious people. A vital instrument for the fulfilment of the missionary vocation of the church is the local congregation.[1]

The WCC world conference on mission and evangelism, held in San Antonio, Texas, in 1989, reminded the ecumenical movement of this all-important but oft-forgotten truth.

Deeply conscious of the churches' own limitations and failures, the conference found itself standing "in awe in the awareness of the belief that God has committed to our faltering faith communities the message of God's love and reign".[2]

To Christians and local congregations who share in this conviction, we offer this booklet as a further encouragement and perhaps also to serve as a practical guide.

We dare name it an "ecumenical evangelistic strategy".

"Strategy", because this booklet is not only about ideas and concepts, it is also about attitudes and methods.

"Ecumenical", because the articulation is the result of many years of listening to the evangelistic stories of many churches belonging to many confessions in many different parts of the world. We have consulted and tested the material with evangelists and teachers in many lands, from Central America to the Middle East, from India and South East Asia to the Sudan, from Aotearoa-New Zealand/Australia to North America and Europe. The encouragement and positive responses, not without criticism by any means, have been strong enough to tempt us to submit this articulation before a much bigger audience in the local churches.

It is "evangelistic" because the strategy aims at ways to awaken or reawaken personal faith in Jesus Christ, and to proclaim to the nations the character and will of God.

We therefore invite your critical scrutiny of this ecumenical strategy for congregation-based evangelism. We urge that you do not take this booklet as a panacea for all the ills of a stagnant congregation, or as a how-to manual on church growth. Such expectations are impossible dreams. They are illusory. If evangelism is anything, it must be local and contextual. We urge you instead to meet the strategy halfway. Are the component elements coherent? Does the strategy make sense in the light of your understanding and experience? Is it productive of further development and will it lead to practical results?

Much theology is involved in composing the ecumenical strategy described in this booklet. We have tried to be explicit and explanatory. We are fully aware that our treatment here is far from thorough. The choice before us was a full-length volume or a more manageable and communicating format. We have opted for the latter. We hope that you will take it not as a finished text crafted in rock but receive it as an invitation for active and considered participation in a generous spirit.

A final point by way of introduction. A local congregation working with this ecumenical strategy will not need a new budget. No extra expenditure is required. We do not make this point as a public-relations gimmick to capture your attention. This point is a theological and missiological given with the strategy. If a local congregation is to share the gospel effectively with every man and woman in the community, every day and all the time, it cannot hope to do so with special funds and special events. It has to be done with its ongoing budget, with its ongoing life and ongoing ministry.

NOTES

[1] Geneva, WCC, 1983, §25.
[2] *The San Antonio Report*, ed. Frederick R. Wilson, Geneva, WCC, 1990, p.35.

The Strategy

There are three elements in this ecumenical strategy.

1. The local congregation, in partnership with other people, pursues the Isaiah Agenda

What is the Isaiah Agenda? It is concrete and clear in its objective. It specifies:
— that children do not die;
— that old people live in dignity;
— that those who build houses live in them;
— and those who plant vineyards eat the fruit.

Isaiah 65:20-23

Our intention is to get involved with people, to work together for the Isaiah Agenda and in the process make sense of Christianity to those who are not interested in Jesus Christ.

We want to communicate the following to our neighbours: "The God we believe in is One who protects the children, enpowers the elderly, and walks with working men and women. As Christians, we wish to act accordingly. We believe you share in similar concerns. Let us join hands."

2. Invitation to worship

As Christians work with children, old folk, working men and women, and with all who share in the Isaiah Agenda, we invite them to worship God with us.

Our intention is to expose our partners in the pursuit of the Isaiah Agenda to an experience of Christian community. To have a taste of it, so to speak, from the inside.

So we say to our neighbours: "Doing the Isaiah Agenda is hard work. There are so many needs, and so many problems. Once in a while, we need to pause. We need to get together, to share our concerns, to celebrate, to pray, to seek strength in order to go on. To worship our God. Would you join us? You know you are most welcome."

3. Invitation to discipleship

In the process of working towards the Isaiah Agenda the partners involved will grow to know and understand each other. Trust and friendship will develop. There will come occasions when it is appropriate for the Christian to invite others to consider the claims of Christ on their lives.

Our intention is to challenge our partners to follow Jesus Christ and to be members of the community of faith.

We seek the opportunity to communicate to our neighbours. "You are invited to be a disciple of Jesus Christ. Whether you are somebody or nobody, rich or poor, powerful or powerless, you are invited to enter into friendship with Jesus and fellowship with the church. You are called to turn around. Take up your cross and follow Jesus, together with us. We are ordinary people called to do extraordinary things with God."

Partnership, worship and discipleship — together these three elements make up this ecumenical evangelistic strategy for the local congregation.

The sequence is relative. Any one of the three elements can be an entry point for evangelistic effort. While they represent different aspects of mission, in the life of a local congregation the three elements flow into one expression of witness, however faltering and imperfect the expression is. There is no one way to evangelize. God loves and reaches out to every individual person in God's own unique and different ways. The Son is the only way to the Father, but there are many ways to Jesus Christ.

An Orthodox community in North Africa began its evangelistic outreach with worship, inviting its neighbours to liturgical prayers. This was followed by the element of partnership with the founding of a community health clinic. The new worshippers participated in the programme as both helpers and the helped. This led to a clear commitment on their part both to church and mission. That is, to discipleship. This process of evangelism is testified to by churches in many denominations. People are exposed to the faith of a Christian community and later on experience and appropriate faith in a personal way.

On the other hand, an equally authentic evangelizing process very often begins with individual conversion outside of a Christian community and moves on to the person's incorporation into a local congregation. In this case, discipleship precedes partnership and worship.

With this understanding of the Holy Spirit's freedom and sovereignty, we recognize that the sequence we follow in this strategy is only relative. But it is not arbitrary. It has a certain logic. It is a response to a very pervasive reality today in which many men and women, old and young, rich and poor, seem to be able to manage their lives reasonably well without Jesus Christ. Among these people a local congregation lives and ministers.

1. The Isaiah Agenda

Of the many biblical visions, why do we go for the Isaiah vision and what Agenda does it provide us?

The Isaiah vision describes what God wants to see happen in human community. It is a community in which:
— children do not die;
— old people live in dignity;
— people who build houses live in them; and
— those who plant vineyards eat the fruit.

Isaiah 65:20-23

This vision calls us to action.

We opt for this particular vision and agenda of the prophet Isaiah because it is biblical, it makes universal sense, it communicates well, it is easy to contextualize, and it is useful as a measure to assess human behaviour, actions and policies. The Isaiah Agenda provides room for every one of us to participate in God's work.

Let us explore the Isaiah Agenda.

Who can hear the Agenda and not understand it? Its utter simplicity is astonishing. But more astonishing is its seemingly immediate relevance for today. However, is such direct application a proper way to read and use scripture? Is it legitimate that we apply this ancient text to our modern world? Perhaps Isaiah 65 refers to the future beyond human history, to the final fulfilment of God's promise. Perhaps the Isaiah Agenda is not meant to be applied to our sinful world of suffering and pain. Perhaps it is God's Agenda only. Doomed to futility is the human effort that attempts to own it.

Objection can also be raised on the ground that Isaiah 65 is rooted in the history of Israel and in Jewish prophecy. It is generally agreed among Old Testament scholars that the text is part of the work of a post-exilic prophet in the tradition of Isaiah of Jerusalem who prophesied in the eighth century before Christ. The immediate audience had knowledge of the exodus and the settlement of the land, as well as of recent history under kings and the experience of the brutal intervention of the great foreign powers. To claim it as a Christian Agenda for a secular and pluralistic world raises exegetical and hermeneutical problems.

These are legitimate questions. But we pledge theological fidelity and ask for missiological freedom. While the whole Isaiah message, 65:8-25, is about judgment, exaltation and restoration, it is nevertheless part of the background for the beatific vision of the New Jerusalem in Revelation 21. Isaiah 65 is not a description of paradise. There is sweat and toil (except that people enjoy the fruit of their labour). There is death and mourning (except that children don't die). The Isaiah Agenda is not about paradise. It has to do with human history, with the here and the now. Our claim is that whatever the biblical context, the Isaiah Agenda expresses God's plan and hope for that human community. God desires that children do not die, that old people live in dignity and that those who work enjoy the fruit of their labour. These constitute part of God's eternal will, testified to in Isaiah 65, but also throughout scripture. To work towards these ends is to do God's will. To work for the Isaiah Agenda is to help make God known to the world. This is the limit of theological capital this ecumenical strategy purposes to draw from the Isaiah text. With boldness, but not without trembling, we dare follow the example of our Lord as he describes his ministry, making use of texts from the book of Isaiah.

While we claim that the Isaiah Agenda, with its concern for children, old people and working men and women, reveals the character of God, we also recognize that it is only a partial revelation. The God whom human beings cannot see is fully revealed only in the person of Jesus Christ. Christians who pursue the Isaiah Agenda need to be fully conscious of its theological limitations, and rejoice in them. Only if we understand and accept that the Isaiah Agenda is a partial revelation of God can we grasp the totality of the ecumenical strategy with its elements of invitation to worship and discipleship.

Further, if we examine the content of the Isaiah Agenda we would have to come to the conclusion that while the Agenda is Christian, it is not Christian in any exclusive sense. It does not represent an inspiration that is available to the Christian faith alone. The Isaiah Agenda comes certainly from a Jewish vision. The Islamic faith can also claim visions like it. So can the statements and manifestos of many political parties and secular governments. Trade unions, chambers of commerce, cooperatives and social service clubs can also be seen to espouse similar causes. If the Isaiah Agenda is a Christian Agenda it is no less a Jewish, Islamic and a secular Agenda. That is the way it is and should be. To us Christians, while we are not naive enough to believe that everyone means the same things with these words, and that basic assumptions and final goals do often differ, that very fact does go to show that God's will is not confined within the boundaries of the Christian church. And this recognition calls for partnership with the world. Christians rejoice over the fact of our non-monopoly.

Another thing we need to understand of the Isaiah Agenda is its modesty. It does not ask for the sky. It calls for what most people nowadays would regard as basic social conditions: children protected, old folk respected, and working men and women given a fair return for their labour. It is a minimum social vision.

There is no reference in it to what most of us nowadays would regard as important — education and career, leisure and vacation, democracy and culture. These good things are of course not excluded from the Isaiah Agenda. They can be drawn out by implication. One can indeed argue that unless human rights are safeguarded institutionally, the Isaiah vision has no long-term viability. But there is no denying that in its stark basic form, the Isaiah Agenda is minimalist in its understanding of human needs. In theological terms, its provisions represent not so much the most that is pleasing to God, but the least that is acceptable to God and therefore to Christians. The Isaiah Agenda is that which every human being has the right to expect of God by virtue of having been brought into the world unasked. People can make the same claim of God's deputies on earth, in governments or in the churches. Children dying, old folk discarded, and workers and peasants going hungry — these things are simply not acceptable in Christian terms. The claims of people are divinely legitimate, and their voices have to be heard.

By the same logic, while the Isaiah Agenda asserts that every working family has a legitimate claim to housing, no one has a claim to a five-bedroom house or a happy home. No one denies that a big house is good and many rooms are desirable. But the Isaiah Agenda would not allow anyone to make a Christian claim on them. Instead we are to humbly recognize them as extras entrusted to us for the blessings of others. Perhaps it is even possible to stop acquiring larger and larger homes for ourselves so that our energies and our resources can be directed to helping the homeless acquire a permanent roof over their heads. With regard to happy homes, the Isaiah Agenda is equally non-promising. Happiness is not entitlement. It is something human beings have to work at, individually and corporately. The Isaiah Agenda provides the bases on which happiness, freedom and community can be built.

So the very modesty of the Isaiah Agenda turns out to have a maximum capacity. Modest as it is, it offers all that is necessary for life, or a new life. The poor understand this. They do not look for a free lunch. They look for the basic conditions to give themselves and their families a real chance in life. The Isaiah Agenda provides them. As for the affluent who already possess all or almost all that the Isaiah Agenda proposes, its modesty provides probably the least modest offer: Give up the petty ambitions and small dreams you have for yourself and your families. Look beyond your petty horizons and dream big. Invest yourself in a cause truly worthy of your calling. In any case, the Agenda's modesty makes it a feasible political proposition.

Another aspect in favour of the Isaiah vision is that it is easy to translate it into action. It is so universal and yet so concrete that any person and any congregation can understand and make something meaningful out of it. Even churches with absolutely no power and hardly any resources can implement some of its objectives.

A mud-thatched congregation in rural Bangladesh keeps a small herd of cattle to provide extra milk to children in the village. Its women's union provides a sense of belonging to sonless widows whose fate otherwise would be social ostracism.

It requires no special expertise to find out why children die. In many places children die because there is no food and they suffer from long-term malnutrition. Many children die of diarrhoea; the water they drink is polluted. Children die of all kinds of preventable diseases because of inadequate primary health care. Children die because of the violence of war, of communal and ethnic conflicts, of gang fights. In some cultures, baby girls are unwanted, and they die of abandonment. We know of millions of children living precariously on city streets. There are situations of environmental pollution so serious that children suffer chronic debilitating diseases of one kind or another. In many circumstances, young lives waste away because of drugs, parental neglect or abuse. We could go on and on. The same with the other elements of the Isaiah Agenda about old people and working men and women.

The Isaiah Agenda is indeed easy to contextualize. All that is required of us is to observe the reality of our situation, ask why, and follow the logic of how things happen in a certain way in our society.

Several congregations in a town in a southern Philippine island gather together to contextualize the Isaiah Agenda. They know that children are prone to die in large numbers in their area. They are malnourished at birth. Their farm-labourer parents cannot bring home enough money to buy decent food for them. This is partly because there are no cooperatives to get them a fair deal. They are divided among themselves. They are made so dependent on the land-owning conglomerates that they cannot get themselves organized. The situation is largely because of the agricultural and export policies which favour the near monopoly of the sugar industry.

The analysis suggests the solutions. Some can be implemented right away and are fairly straightforward. Community day care. Nutrition counselling. A simple food bank. A primary health team of volunteers. Other solutions would take much time and involve more risk for the congregations. For example a decision to help organize local farm labourers. This means seeking training and expertise, and getting in touch with national cooperatives and farmers' movements. The congregations also write urgent letters to the national offices of their churches and urge high-level advocacy in order to influence government economic policies in favour of the poor. They pledge their readiness to get involved in any meaningful church-wide effort towards this.

Obviously a local congregation cannot do everything to ensure that children do not die. But it can do a lot where it is, and a great deal more if it joins hands with other congregations and others of good will. It can certainly cry out, loudly and clearly, that whoever and whatever causes children to die violates the will of God and works against our own future. Such a message will bring comfort and encouragement to the poor and to all people of good will. It will be judgment and challenge to those in the corridors of power.

Finally, the beauty of the Isaiah Agenda is that every person can play a part in it and contribute to it. Simple acts of personal kindness and mercy. Corporate efforts to relieve pain and suffering. Political action to challenge unjust structures. As long as they contribute to the Isaiah Agenda in some way, they contribute to the doing of God's will and to the fulfilment of the mission of the church. Every person in the congregation can do something, however limited and humble, however frail and feeble it may appear. Each stands equally tall in the task of making God better known.

2. Invitation to Worship

Regular involvement in the Isaiah Agenda will have two immediate consequences for the church.

First we get to know many people in the area in which we live and work. We get to know many children, old people and working men and women, as well as their families and their friends. We also get to know people who, even if they do not share our understanding of the basis of the Isaiah Agenda nevertheless wish to support it in various ways. They are people who'd like to help.

The Isaiah vision represents a universal aspiration, however limited it is as a social reality in many places. The more the congregation is involved in the Agenda the more people it will get to know, and the more extensive will become the contacts it will have in the community. The church itself will also become known. Soon, we can expect the occasional privilege of people coming to us.

Second, pursuing the Isaiah Agenda is no easy job. It takes a lot out of us physically and emotionally. If we mean business, we will inevitably find ourselves asking one day: "What has the world come to that with all the resources the world has at its command and the tremendous progress it claims to have made, children are still dying in large numbers, old folk are increasingly left to their own fate, and working people go on getting a poor deal?" No doubt we may experience occasional support and friendship and even come across uplifting heroism. But we will never be able to escape from the weight of human indifference, selfishness, greed, stupidity and hypocrisy in the face of human suffering. The Isaiah Agenda is too much for us, for anyone.

These two consequences point to one answer: worship and the invitation to worship. In worship, as Christians we gather up our involvement in the Isaiah Agenda and offer it to God. In worship, we celebrate Jesus Christ who died and rose for us and who walks with us, shares our burdens and saves us. In worship, we are reminded once again that we do not labour alone, and that we are a community which supports one another. The more involved Christians are in the Isaiah Agenda the more our need for worship. If we think we can make any headway with the Isaiah Agenda without a regular worship life, we are fooling ourselves. Many Christians do, unfortunately. They get burned out. They become so weighed down that they are no good to themselves and to others. Involvement in the Isaiah Agenda drives us to worship. And, since we are at that, why not, as well, invite our Isaiah Agenda partners to join us? Invitation to worship, the second element in our ecumenical strategy.

The Isaiah Agenda makes visible something of the God whom human beings cannot see. It reveals what God is like, to some extent. But there is a great deal more about God that it does not reveal. In worship one gets to hear about Jesus, in whose person God is fully revealed.

And, what may be even more important, one gets to know more about God from within, from inside a community of faith. Experiencing from inside is always different from standing on the outside looking in.

To some Christians, the idea of inviting our Isaiah Agenda partners and friends to worship with us is highly problematic. It could be embarrassing. The worship services in many of our churches are often either so uninspiring and clannish, or so unintelligent and unintelligible — or both — that we'd rather not invite others. If that is the case, we have a real problem on our hands.

Many churches have now recognized the seriousness of the situation. The revitalization of worship is high on the church's agenda.

How can we have the kind of worship to which we are not embarrassed to bring our partners and friends? Indeed, how can we have the kind of worship that may expose others to an experience of God?

The first thing to realize is that worship is not a means to evangelism. It is not something Christians do in order that some good, however it is defined, will happen to other people. Worship is our way to God and at the same time our celebration of the love of God. The key to authentic worship is the presence of authentic worshippers. They transform the most routine liturgies into encounters with the love and glory of God.

So our question is not how to make worship more appealing to people outside of the churches in order to attract them to our midst. The question is how Christians worship together authentically. If we do, we can be assured that our partners and friends may also experience God in some way in and through our service of worship.

Involvement in the Isaiah Agenda helps make better worshippers of Christians. It makes us sensitive to the reality around us, and to our own limitations. And sometimes it surprises us with joy when unexpected good things come out of very feeble human efforts. Our involvement in the Isaiah Agenda deepens our hunger for God, feeds our desire for God's intervention in our own lives and in the lives of others. In such a state of mind, we encounter God in worship.

It is important that a worship service takes note of two things.

First, it must embrace the everyday concerns of the worshippers. They need to know that the things they care about from Monday to Saturday, God also cares about. That their lives which intersect with children, old people, and working men and women are points of mission where God is at work, and where transformation of lives, ours and others', can happen. However mundane our lives and witness, they are the concerns of the church, and are fit topics for corporate caring and reflection, intercession and thanksgiving. A mother concerned about her unemployed son and his friends should feel as free to bring the matter to the attention of the congregation as she would feel free to bring news of an old man who has become seriously sick. And she should be able to bring up the matter not as a private request and a case for welfare, but as a corporate concern and a case for missionary engagement.

Secondly, and following on the first, while worship embraces the cares and concerns of our mundane living, it does not deal with them primarily on the level of human relationships, economics or politics. Christians do not assemble to vent the grievances of yesterday and today. We do not use the occasion to indulge in our own political preferences. We meet to reaffirm our faith in the sovereignty of our great and compassionate God "who is able to keep us from falling, and to present us faultless before the presence of his glory with exceeding joy". Such a worship is authentic and, for that very reason, truly evangelistic.

To convey this sense of the divine embrace of daily living, in the awareness of God's love and power, all elements of worship should be brought into play — music and singing, announcements, preaching, testimonies, intercessions, silences. We already have the right ingredients in our worship. Let us set them to work.

The practical business of actually attempting to design an act of worship that is authentic and inviting is beyond the competence of this booklet written for an international audience. So much is dependent on ecclesiastical traditions, confessional positions, sociology and culture, and even the temperament of the people involved. The most we can do here is to share a few broad observations.

— Established orders of worship are used for a good reason. They have proved themselves adequate, at least for one time. Stay with the one you have and work for improvement within it.

— If change must come about, go about it seriously. Study, try out a few variations, and stay with one format. Renewal in worship doesn't mean a new order of worship every Sunday. People need to be accustomed to a liturgical pattern so that they can turn their attention to God rather than having to struggle to find their way through an unfamiliar sequence.

— Not all traditional anthems are wordy and dull. Not all scriptural choruses are biblical and inspiring. Not all Taizé chants are duplicable and transferable. Not all evangelical hymns are sentimental and individualistic. But one thing is always important: a good and humble song leader, or a small team; that helps.

— As for the sermon, the preacher's words, before they can become word to the congregation, have first to become word to himself or herself in the privacy of sermon preparation. The same goes for intercessory prayers and testimonies. People can tell the difference.

— Throughout the service, use words in such a way that leaves room for the people to respond meditatively. What is audible in a worship service is not the entire service, only a part. Do not feel you must spell out everything. Leave room for the Holy Spirit. Let God control the space between transmission and reception.

In the multicultural society that most of us live in today, it is entirely conceivable that what is experienced as authentic by some Christians is felt to be alien by others. It is not hard to envisage people of different ethnic origins, and young people, finding it difficult to fit into a certain way of worship.

I believe the church should accept this and start with this recognition. The burden of taking initiatives lies with those in power. Many churches have opted for a second worship service with a different style at a different hour on Sunday.

Whatever the circumstances, the most important goal remains a worship which embraces the daily involvement of the Christians, deals with it in the light of God's power and love, and communicates God's blessing and honour to all those involved.

Up to now, we have been speaking of worship in terms of the regular Sunday service of the local congregation.

This is as it should be. But for this ecumenical strategy, the invitation to worship includes also other occasions of brief duration outside of church buildings. These could be short litanies to begin or conclude a social event, simple symbolic acts at points of crisis. They could also be more organized events such as home fellowship groups. The important thing is to make use of natural occasions of worship where our Isaiah Agenda partners may experience God within a Christian community.

An inner-city church worker in Wichita, Kansas, tells of this experience. Venture House is an Episcopalian social service reaching out to the city's down and out. "Mary was a 'bag lady', homeless, ill with several physical and mental problems. She had turned to Venture House for help. Since then she had come to know all of the staff and many of the volunteers. She had also heard that they prayed. One day, she shyly asked a volunteer worker to have them pray for her. 'Mary, why don't you come by early tomorrow and pray with us?' the volunteer invited. Next day happened to be a dreary, overcast Good Friday morning. Mary came and sat quietly, observing these people at prayer. A volunteer read the gospel appointed for that day. As he read about the death of Jesus, the attention of staff and volunteers was fixed on the sadness of the words. When the man finished, silence permeated the room. Mary broke the silence by saying to the group, 'You know, if there are people like you in the world, perhaps Jesus really was raised from the dead.'"

Small Christian communities existing in slums have always found it liberating to conclude their gatherings with their neighbours with a short litany. Whether their neighbours are secular people or adherents of other faiths, a short prayer to God or a simple litany gives an added dimension to their relationship, a deeper sense of fellowship and of individual well-being.

The same is being discovered by well-off people in the West and in urban centres. Through house parties and luncheon gatherings, Christians in business and in the professions have been able to achieve a deeper sense of friendship with their secular colleagues which does not exclude the sharing of personal needs. A lay movement which has contributed to the founding of many churches among the business communities in Malaysia and Thailand in recent years has found the following format effective.

Two or three Christians work together to invite their business colleagues to a house party or a luncheon at a hotel. It is a normal social gathering. Ten or fifteen minutes before the end, one of the hosts would stand up and suggest a topic for conversation. On this occasion, it is "How has my business affected my family life?" Another host would respond with his or her own experience. Soon, the guests would also start sharing. The party or luncheon concludes with a short and simple prayer which commits all the families represented to God's care. In many cases, this is the beginning of interest in the Christian faith. Samples of useful topics: What are your gifts? What are your goals in life? What are the needs in society today that you can make a contribution to? Which people have influenced your life the most?

Not everyone will accept our invitation to worship. Perhaps only a few will. That is all right. Christians worship regularly, week after week. And ours is a standing invitation, personally renewed at discreet intervals. There are also situations where the law of the land discourages such invitations to worship. But, even then, we recognize that this is but one element out of a three-element strategy. The Isaiah Agenda also communicates God. And our involvement is permanent.

Worship evangelizes precisely by being, and remaining, worship. It is not a tool for evangelism, just as our involvement in the Isaiah Agenda is not a means of evangelism. But together they help make God better known to the world.

3. Invitation to Discipleship

In the course of our daily involvement with children, old people, working men and women, and others of good will, and during the more heightened occasions of corporate worship, there will come moments when some of our partners and friends stand poised, ready to express an awakened personal faith in Jesus Christ. When such moments arise, Christians should not hesitate to issue an invitation to discipleship. It could happen in a face-to-face encounter. It could be an altar call. It could be a summons to the eucharist. It could be a simple announcement in the church bulletin of classes for those seeking baptism. Whatever our approach, the important thing is that Christians remain sensitive to signs of the awakening and the reawakening of personal faith, and issue an invitation to discipleship. The third and final element in this ecumenical evangelistic strategy.

There are Christians who find it difficult to invite others. They have little difficulty talking about the Isaiah Agenda but when it comes to matters of personal faith, they are tongue-tied.

Much of this reluctance has to do with personal temperament and cultural difference. We don't want to intrude on the privacy of others. We fear embarrassment. We want to be sensitive.

However, when the signs of awakening faith are perceived, it is precisely because of the requirement of sensitivity that Christians invite. Not to invite would be insensitive. For the heart of the matter is, to be Christian is not to join a social club. To be Christian is to be a disciple of Jesus, to follow Christ. It profoundly affects a person's values. What used to be important may not now look so important. What used to be taken for granted is now brought into question. Conversion affects our orientation, our loyalties and relationships. To be Christian is to start living a new life. Nowadays, in most societies, the act of following Jesus does not necessarily involve suffering or hardship. In some societies it still does, from experiencing discrimination in education and career to imprisonment and martyrdom. But, however and wherever we look at it, becoming a Christian is a very serious matter, certainly for the person concerned.

If becoming a Christian is indeed such a serious matter affecting behaviours, attitudes and values, indeed one's very identity, it stands to reason that the person to be affected should be given at least the courtesy of personal attention. Given the likely consequences, he or she is entitled to a clear, personal invitation from God or from whoever claims to speak in God's name. No general invitation will do. No welcome-mat at the entrance of a church can ever do justice to what is asked of the person. He or she is entitled to a specific invitation, personal and by name. "You are invited to be a disciple of Jesus Christ." Anything less would be callous, disrespectful and unjust.

The writer recalls his conversion experience during his student days. If becoming a Christian is likened to going to a banquet, I would most probably not have gone into the banquet hall, not without an invitation which clearly was addressed to me by name. However tempting the food, however wide open the door, I must have a personal invitation from the host before I go in. Lest I am less than welcome. Lest I misread the signals. There was too much at stake. I could not afford a mistake.

What do we as Christians actually communicate to our partners and friends of the Isaiah Agenda when we invite them to discipleship?

We try to communicate the same things as Jesus did when he called people to follow him in his day. He has one basic message, expressed in different ways according to the needs of the person and the prevailing circumstances. His message to would-be disciples was simple: "Take up your own cross and follow me." This too must be our message today. This is the content of our invitation to discipleship.

By this formulation, Christians communicate the following to children, old people, working men and women, and all people of good will — our partners and friends in the Isaiah Agenda:

— You are invited to friendship with Jesus.
— You are invited to community, a community of those who follow Christ.
— You are invited to repentance, to a new direction, so turn away from your old ways.
— You are invited to assume responsibility for your life and indeed to be a blessing to others. You are invited to reject self-pity and resignation. The crucified and risen Lord has already inaugurated God's kingdom in human history. The disciples are part of that kingdom. You are invited to assume responsibility for your life not because the law of man says you are responsible, but because the grace of God has given you the power to be responsible. With Jesus, and in the company of fellow Christians, you can take hold of your own life, and much more.
— We are but ordinary people, but we have been invited to do extraordinary things with God.

This is our message. This is what Christians communicate to their partners and friends of the Isaiah Agenda. We do not have different messages for different people. To rich and poor, to young and old, to the strong and the frail, to the religious and the secular, we dare say: "Regardless of who you are or who you think you are, you are invited to be a disciple of Jesus Christ."

Can we prove all our claims? Can Christians, for instance, prove that Jesus Christ is the Son of God? That he walked the face of the earth, died and rose again, for our liberation and salvation? Most probably not. Not in propositional terms, for sure. But that is not our job. Our job is not to prove that Jesus Christ is the Son of God. Our job is to show to the satisfaction of others that we believe he is.

Not all will respond. But that does not matter. Our job is not to convert people into disciples. Our job is to issue the invitation. And let us not forget our other job, involvement in the Isaiah Agenda together with children, old people, working men and women, and all persons of good will. The church continues to uphold the Isaiah vision before the eyes of the community:

Never again will there be in it an infant that lives but a few days,
or an old man who does not live out his years;
They will build houses and live in them;
They will plant vineyards and eat their fruit...

For as the days of a tree,
So will be the days of my people...

Before they call I will answer;
While they are still speaking I will hear...

This is the God Christians invite others to follow.

Attitudes,
Spirituality,
Methods

How can Christian involvement in the Isaiah Agenda be a Christian witness and not only humanitarian or social-political action, good as that is? How can it reveal God?

How can our invitation to worship and discipleship be truly inviting?

Indeed, how can this three-pronged strategy evangelize?

It is entirely conceivable that a congregation goes through the motions of all three elements of the ecumenical strategy and no one for all the trouble becomes any wiser about God and the ways of God. I am exaggerating. But Christians know that one can have the finest strategies, the best thought-through message and the most appropriate actions, and hearts remain untouched, unmoved. Our strategy, message and action stay empty and powerless.

It is time we deal with that which is within us which gives the crucial and decisive nuances to what we say and do.

Sometimes we call "that which is within us" our basic convictions — beliefs that are held deep in our being which inform our every thought and every deed.

Sometimes we call it attitude — the inclination to act. Attitude is the bridge between the idea and the action. Two persons acting on the same idea may generate very different responses from the same people, although the format of their action is similar. The decisive difference lies in attitude.

And, where our convictions and our inclination to act are a response to the Holy Spirit, we call it spirituality.

Whatever we call it — convictions, attitudes or spirituality, it determines whether our actions in pursuit of the Isaiah Agenda and our invitations to worship and discipleship evangelize or do not evangelize.

What follows is a discussion of the how-to's of evangelism on this internal, spiritual level. We want to describe the kind of life within which, evangelistically, we can inform and shape our external involvement in the Isaiah vision and in our invitations. We also want to discuss the methods consistent with such attitudes and spirituality.

1. God Is Present and at Work

How do we Christians see the world around us? What is our theological assessment of the human situation? Our answer determines to a very large extent how we understand ourselves and other people in our day-to-day encounters.

We believe that God is present among people and at work in the world. Even where there is no perceptible Christian witness, God is not absent.

Often the signs of God's presence in the world are unclear to us. Sin and evil can so blur the signs that they cannot always be noticed. There are times when the signs are so distorted and abused that the God they point to in fact shows up to be someone or something totally different. But for the Christian, the conviction remains that God is alive and is at work. The world has sinned but is not abandoned. People who don't know God through Jesus Christ are lost but are not forsaken. God is at work, even where there is no Christian church. God is present even before Christians appear on the scene.

People of good will must certainly include persons of other living faiths. Among them, God is also present and at work.

There has been in recent years much serious debate in theological circles on the question of how Christians understand the theological significance of other faiths. My first inclination is to decline to discuss the question on the ground of my respect for other faiths. If we apply Christian criteria and Christian categories to faiths which do not claim to be Christian, we can never do them justice. We are bound to find them less than adequate. If I take myself as the standard and then proceed to measure other people, everyone else will be either too short or too tall. Christians need to understand and respect their Buddhist, Muslim and Hindu neighbours on their own terms.

However, the question of the theological significance of other faiths remains a crucial academic issue as well as an existential concern in daily life. We cannot help but observe and make our judgment from where we are. In what sense then is God present and at work in other living faiths? In some theological circles, there is talk about the saving presence of God in other faiths and their saving values. I am ready to go a long way in affirming God's presence in other living faiths. But to say that a certain faith has saving values is not to say that it can indeed save. I as an Asian may be able to own a lot of African values, but I can never be an African. God is present and at work among people of other living faiths, as God is present and at work on this planet of ours.

This explains, from the Christian perspective, the universality of the Isaiah vision as a human aspiration. Even the most self-centred cultures, the most secular and commercialized societies, atheistic regimes and totalitarian states, and even the poorest nations, produce some Isaiah Agenda results. Some more, some less, in a manner that is meant to meet their needs. To the Christian, this is a sign of God being at work, an encouragement to join God's bandwagon, and a reason to work with all people of good will.

The Isaiah Agenda shows clearly that all peoples and all human systems have come short. This is reason for critique and action. But it should never translate into a permanent outlook of hostility on the part of the Christian. A habitual disposition of criticism against the world because paradise has not yet arrived indicates an unfulfilled, unattractive life. Christians who are disposed that way may do a lot of good as they work for the Isaiah Agenda, but the God they reveal cannot be very attractive.

So let Christians rejoice that God is at work in the world. Let us be appreciative of the fumbling human efforts towards the Isaiah Agenda and give credit where it is due. Such efforts too are a response to God's presence. Let us take comfort in the thought that God has the crucial role, and we play no more than the second fiddle. Let us be grateful that the burden of the world does not fall on our shoulders. As the well-known spiritual tells us, "He's got the whole world in his hands". In this way, our involvement in the Isaiah Agenda is light and joyful and it points to God.

The conviction that God is present and at work empowers us. Our resources are limited. Our power is insignificant. Yet we are faced with the million horrors of children losing their young lives, of old folk dying long before their bodies wither away, and working men and women finding it increasingly hard to make ends meet. How can we realistically make a difference? The forces opposing the Isaiah Agenda appear strong and intransigent. Is it not a case of David and Goliath?

Precisely. For change is not our business. Our role is not to create change. We cannot. Our role is to influence change, so that people and things change for the better and not for the worse. Christians influence change, making it faster, steering it towards more justice, more peace and a more healthy and human environment. Given this more modest role, our limited resources and insignificant power can assume a magnitude they do not have in themselves. A David can indeed defeat a Goliath. God is behind him.

The key lies in our conviction of God's presence in the world and our discernment of where the Holy Spirit is moving. Then we place ourselves, our limited resources and powers, where God is at work and become God's co-workers.

While I was working in urban mission in the city of Hong Kong, I came to know a group of textile workers, mostly young women in their early twenties. They worked in the same plant and occasionally would gather for an evening of fun. About Christmas time, although only two out of the thirty were Christians, the group decided to do something "Christian". They settled on doing a Bible study on the Lukan version of the first Christmas. The

Christians were very excited. They got in touch with us and made a detailed study plan with background material and questions for discussion and so on. But nothing like that happened. Once the young women got into Luke 2, most of them reading the Bible for the first time, they refused to follow our well-thought-out scheme. They were captured by one idea in the Christmas narrative — that Mary, the mother of Jesus, in pregnancy, had to travel a long distance, risking her health and the life of her baby. This was the point on which the young women's attention focused. They would not be drawn away. Immediately they identified themselves with Mary. Like the mother of Jesus, they too had the experience of having their health and their yet-to-be-born babies put at risk because of the need to stay on the job until the last possible day. They were fascinated that Mary had to go through the same hardship. I could see their eyes brighten up. Their very mundane experience, to which nobody in Hong Kong gave a second thought, which even the poor themselves took for granted, is in fact the experience of the mother of Jesus. How can it be? Are we after all so important?

At the time, labour legislation in Hong Kong provided for maternity leave, but without pay. So the law was totally meaningless. No working-class woman could afford to claim the leave. As a matter of fact, many women workers in the late months of their pregnancy would work overtime in order to save enough to tide over the post-delivery period when they could not work. The young women shared their experience and those of their friends. For the first time, they saw themselves in the world of Mary and Jesus. They realized that what they cared about, the Bible also cares about. Luke 2 did not provide a solution to the problem of pregnant workers. What Luke 2 did was to embrace these workers and affirm their concerns.

The solution was obvious — to fight for an amendment to the existing law, to make the provision of maternity leave a paid provision. Thus began an organized effort by women workers to change the law. In ten months, the law was changed to provide two-thirds of the regular wages.

It was a costly struggle in every sense. Many in the group dedicated all their hours apart from work to rally support, to visit hospitals, to compile data, to speak to the press, to appear on television, to present their case to lawmakers. Every single step had to be learned and every sentence memorized. Everyone endured tremendous pressure from friends, husbands, parents. "What is a simple woman like you doing in politics, making a fool of yourself in the open?" A number dropped out and then came back in. Three gave up altogether. And when the young women gathered, there was sometimes tension among them. Some felt their burdens were too heavy, that others had not done their part. Others felt misunderstood. There was much prayer and there were many conversions. But the conversion also brought unforeseen problems. Three of the leaders who were baptized began to have doubts at one point. A Christian employers' group joined the chamber of commerce to oppose the legislative amendment. These Christian employers urged the workers to withdraw their effort for the wellbeing of the city. Paid maternity leave would drive up cost, harm our export, frighten investors, hurt our economy — and ordinary people would suffer. A prominent pastor echoed similar sentiments. The new converts were torn in their convictions. It was indeed a costly struggle.

But support soon developed. A few more churches joined the drive. A few more labour unions. The YWCA. The League of Women Lawyers. The largest Christian hospitals eventually came out in support because they knew women workers suffered a higher-than-average rate of still births. Actually, they knew all along. In ten months, the law was changed. And many lives were changed also.

So the word of God came to a few vulnerable, powerless persons, and transformed them into a people. They in turn were able to help the city discover that it did have a soul.

The textile workers who lobbied successfuly for paid maternity leave in the city of Hong Kong did not create that change. They influenced it. There was already a degree of readiness in the city for more just labour legislation. New political, economic and social realities had come into being and were in a state of preparedness. The government was blind to it. Most business interests fought against it. The Christian churches were too apathetic to read the signs. It took an encounter of a group of young women workers with Luke 2 to bring out this piece of new reality deep in the soul of the city. What the women did was to bring out this readiness, which the city eventually recognized as its own.

So the conviction that God is present and at work enpowers us. When we discern where the Holy Spirit is moving, we would know where to be. In a chess game, a humble pawn can beat the powerful queen, if placed right. It is a matter of articulation. We can be a lone voice crying in the wilderness. But ours can also be one that finds an echo in thousands of human hearts. It is a matter of timing. It is no less a matter of speaking the truth that the emperor has no clothes. A matter of discernment that the formidably armoured giant has feet of clay. Our God is present and at work.

2. In Partnership with the World

While God plays the most important role in the drama of the Isaiah vision, Christians play a secondary role. But we are not the only supporting actors. There are others. The local congregation should see itself as a partner with the people in the community. Children, old folk, working men and women and their families are our partners. So are the schools, the village elders, the neighbourhood committees, the cooperatives, the trade unions, the chambers of commerce, government departments, professional bodies — in short, everybody and every organization which has anything to do with the Isaiah Agenda. We are partners with one another.

What does it mean for the church to be a partner? Let us first look at what partnership is not.

A partner is not a saviour or messiah. The church does not save. Jesus Christ does. Christians do not carry the sins of the world on their back. Jesus Christ did and he did it once and for all. The Christian's role is much more modest. We point people to Christ: Behold, the Lamb of God. We should never pretend otherwise. Our neighbours never think of Christians as saviours anyway. They would accept us as we are — very imperfect fellow human beings who have some experience of God.

A partner is not a Santa Claus. A Santa Claus is one who distributes freebies to everyone. He is a jolly, good grandpa figure too nice to ever say no. The days of the power and wealth of Christendom have long since gone. And while the church still has resources through the giving of its people, most of us have come to realize that charity is not always helpful and paternalism breeds dependency, resentment and manipulation. A congregation which behaves like a Santa Claus can do many things. Some of these may be good. But the one thing a Santa Claus figure cannot do is to challenge the recipient of his goodies to change and to follow in the footsteps of Jesus. Only a partner who walks alongside his or her neighbours and shares in their joy and sorrow can do that.

→ Christ as
servant?

A partner is not a servant. A servant has no will of his
or her own. A servant does the will of the master. This
means while we as Christians may understand ourselves as
servants to God, we are not servants to other people and to
the world.

This is not an easy thing to say to the church. The
language of servanthood has become very much part of
our mission language. Christians like to think and speak in
these terms. They are surely biblical expressions and
biblical concepts. But are they useful today? Do they
communicate to our partners and friends who are outside
of the churches the relevance and urgency of the Isaiah
Agenda? The answer is obviously no.

Several years ago, it was popular in some Christian
circles to say that "the world sets the agenda of the
church". Now nobody says that any more. While the
expression properly understood could well be true in a
profound sense, as it stands it no longer holds water. It is
silly, even hypocritical, to suggest and to imply that the
church does not have its own agenda.

Obviously, this agenda should be humbly offered and
clearly presented before the world. If the agenda makes
sense to others, we rejoice. If it coincides with that of
others of good will, all the better. But an agenda the
church certainly has, not in any possessive sense but in the
sense of a partner offering his or her best available
contribution to a partnership. And with no apologies.

As it is, to describe the church as servant to the world
is clearly inadequate. It sounds as if the church does not
know what it is about, where it is going or what message it
has for the world. This may well be true, unfortunately,
with certain churches, in which case there is all the more
reason to do away with the "servant" language.

In any case, the world knows only too well today that
the church neither looks nor sounds like "servant". This
could be taken as legitimate criticism. But at this point I
mean it as a factual observation. A California-based multi-

million dollar international Christian group defines itself as "servant to the poor". While the organization means well, the designation strains credibility. It makes sense only to the piety and good intentions of those responsible for the organization. Admittedly, this is an extreme case. But by and large, the same is not untrue of most local congregations. With its membership, programmes and buildings, it is hard to think of many a local congregation in the image of servant to the community. If the congregation is open and available to the community, it is not because it has been ordered to be so, like a servant, but because it has freely decided to. Its openness and availability are the expression of the will of people who have decided to be so. And the neighbours know that.

Even in circumstances where the Christian church is a small and persecuted minority, with absolutely no social and institutional power, the servant image still does hardly apply. Simply by existing as a worshipping community around the word of God and the sacraments, the local congregation exults in its role, assuming the strength and dignity of people resisting the pressure to conform.

The concept of the church as servant to the world no longer communicates today. It does not do justice to the role of the church in mission. It fails to match the church's present-day realities, whether in a good or a bad sense. We need a new language to enable us to think afresh and with clarity, and to communicate to the world with honesty and with invitation.

The new language proposed in this ecumenical strategy for Christian witness is partnership. The local congregation sees itself as a partner with the people in the community, and offers itself publicly as such.

Partners are equals. Partners know their limits and limitations, recognizing the share they are bound to contribute. A partner expects other partners to give their fair share. A partner knows that without others, he or she cannot succeed. A partner does not do things for other partners. They do things together. Partners share gain and loss. They share joy and sorrow.

A partner has his or her own favourite agenda, but does not impose it on the other partners. Partners share their agenda with one another and they are in dialogue. They agree on some things but do not need to agree on all things. They do some things together but do not need to do all things together. But the recognition of partnership compels them to explain their convictions to each other honestly and humbly. Partners are answerable to one another. They are mutually accountable.

A partner also serves his or her fellow partners beyond the call of duty as the need arises. In a partnership, one does not serve because one is a servant. One serves because one is not a servant. And the service is that much more meaningful and treasured precisely because it is not the service of servants but the service of equals.

The concept of partnership is a distinct and unmistakeable echo of Jesus' way of dealing with his fumbling followers. Towards the end of his ministry, Jesus gathered his disciples and told them many things. At one point, he said to them: "I no longer call you servants because a servant does not know his master's business, instead I have called you friends; for everything that I learned from my Father, I have made known to you" (John 15:15).

Making known to others what one knows — this is the distinctive feature of a partnership. That is why evangelism requires that Christians strive to place themselves in a position of partners with people outside the church. They are in fact the permanent constituencies of the Christian church to whom the church is answerable.

Partnership, however, is a two-way affair. We cannot be partners with others if others do not want to be partners with us. What about the fact of human sinfulness? Are human beings not rebels in opposition to God's way, the Isaiah Agenda included? That human beings are in a state of rebellion against God is a theological fact. But it does not make the Christian call to partnership mere romanticism. Rebels are not strangers to God. They are reacting to something. Christians do not consider persons of no faith or other faiths as having no relation to God, or no experience of the transcendent. Who can fathom the depth of the human heart?

The sav~~ing grace of God is not only offered to all,~~ it is ~~promised to all~~. This makes it difficult for Christians to approach people as total aliens, as if they have absolutely no sense of the experience and vision that we treasure. On the contrary, we address everyone we meet as a potential follower of Christ, as a person who will one day confess and live by God's saving grace. With such expectancy, based on our conviction of God's convincing grace, we issue the invitation to partnership, worship and discipleship.

Will the people respond to the Christian offer of partnership, worship and discipleship?

Dom Helder Camara, a much-loved bishop in Brazil, knows they will. "If we don't press the absurd claim of being the best, if we present ourselves as brothers and sisters for others, we shall be astounded to discover what a lot of people of good will there are about. Some of them may perhaps be rather timid, others will be so situated that they can't see things in the same light as we do. But once they come across somebody who speaks from the heart, not seeking to impose anything on them or humiliate them, and not with the conviction of being any cleverer or holier, then they are affected and would also join the march."[1]

In a Central American city, a congregation has been running a very fine programme among children in a nearby slum. But the money runs out. The church can no longer pay the youth worker. What is to be done? Close the programme? Seek help from churches in the West? The church people and the youth worker decide to tell the children, about seventy of them, and their parents about it. The church has never done such a thing before. The church has gathered them for all kinds of celebrations and educational sessions, but never to share its problems and to seek their help. What is the point? These people are poor. They cannot even feed their families.

But on this occasion the church decided to expose its problems and its needs to the poor to whom it ministers. And the young people and their parents responded. Some of their responses were not easy. They started raising questions about the church having run out of money. Some parents sat down with the pastor going through the church budget and asking: "Is this item really important? Can we not move fifty dollars from here to the youth worker's salary?" There was a lot of give and take. The parents decided to raise some money. The young people decided to raise some money too, doing it all on their own. Many youngsters and adults participated in the prayer meetings of the church for the continuation of the programme. Hitherto, no adults from the slum had ever attended the Sunday worship of that church. They had been happy and content enjoying the help rendered by the church on the weekdays. Now many started coming to worship on Sundays.

A church communicating strength and power can be a provider of many useful services, but only a church that is not afraid of communicating weakness and need can draw people to God and build them up as full participants in the community of faith. That indeed is at the root of the methodology and spirituality of partnership.

NOTE

[1] *Through the Gospel with Dom Helder Camara*, Maryknoll, NY, Orbis, 1986, p.109.

3. Sharing in Solidarity

When we get involved with children, old folk and others, in the Isaiah Agenda, there will come to us many occasions of sharing. Sharing of experience, ideas, in action and waiting, of money and material things. In short, partnership with the world within the discipline of the Isaiah Agenda suggests a continuous process of sharing. So it is important that Christians examine how they share. Sharing is good, but not always easy. Sharing across economic, cultural and racial boundaries requires special sensitivity.

We do not see Christian sharing as an evangelistic tool, a way to get people into the church. Far from it. We understand sharing as so much of a Christian calling in itself that we want to make sure our sharing empowers people and does not make them dependent, safeguards human dignity and does not humiliate those who receive, builds trust and understanding and not resentment and hatred. The Christian desire to give food to a hungry child, to spend time with a lonely old man, and to lend political support to working people struggling for fair wages and decent housing comes from the same desire as that of sharing with them the gospel of Jesus Christ.

How then do we share ? There are generally two ways. One is that we share out of a sense of generosity. We have, while others have not. We are developed while others are underdeveloped. We are privileged while others are less privileged. We reach out to others because we are different from them.

This is a worthy motive. Perhaps even a Christian motive. And many acts of philanthropy have been undertaken on this basis. On the other hand, the same generosity has often been turned into an excuse to perpetuate injustice, domination and paternalism. Sharing out of a sense of generosity, in any case, is sharing from a distance, because it is based on perceived difference. This is not a position from which anyone can issue the invitation to worship and discipleship and expect an authentic response.

The other way is the way poor people share among themselves — out of a sense of solidarity. We share because we understand and feel the pain of others. We reach out not because we are different but because we are no different. We see ourselves in the suffering of others. We remember the pains of our own past. We drop our pretences and dare face our real selves. So we share. People know the difference between the two ways. And they respond accordingly.

Solidarity, I believe, is the more biblical way. The people of Israel are reminded of their duty towards strangers. "You shall not oppress a stranger; you know the heart of a stranger, for you were strangers in the land of Egypt" (Ex. 23:8). It was an appeal based not on perceived difference, but on perceived common history. The same is the case with Paul's reminder to the early church: "Treat your servants justly and fairly, knowing you also have a master in heaven" (Col. 4:1, Eph. 6:8). Be just to your servant because you too are a servant. If Christians see themselves this way, there will be no arrogance and no paternalism in our dealings with the poor and the powerless. How can there be if we come to realize that we too are poor and powerless in the eyes of God? And if we are poor and powerless in the eyes of God, we are truly and really so indeed.

Here we come to the theological heart of the matter. Here we come to understand why sharing in solidarity is a more Christian attitude. As we pursue the Isaiah Agenda, amidst the powerlessness of children and old people, and side by side with men and women struggling for their daily bread, their reality will, like a mirror, show us as never before our own poverty and powerlessness.

And this is good. This is good because blessed are the poor, for theirs is the kingdom of God. If Christians share in solidarity and understand their own poverty, they would not lose their soul in the very act of trying to save others. On the contrary, they will become, as in the now famous definition of evangelism from Asia, the blessed beggar to whom other beggars come to find out where food can be found.

Christmas. It is the season of sharing gifts and toys with the children. But not for the children in the slum. Their parents have no money to buy them toys. So for this particular congregation it is time for their members to start collecting toys, toys from middle-class homes and from their sister congregations in the suburbs. This year, however, this congregation has done something different. Instead of giving the toys directly to the children, the members devise a plan to have the parents buy those toys at a tiny fraction of the cost. They have seen that when they handed over the toys to the children, the children were overjoyed, but the parents were embarrassed. The more the children boasted of their toys to each other, the more ashamed were their parents.

The church that gives away toys to children may be able to draw the children to the church, but it keeps the parents away. Sharing should not have the effect of taking their dignity away from people. Sharing should not keep people away from the community of faith. So the Christians in this church devise the plan. They collect many old toys. They invite the parents from the slum to come in to clean and to mend these toys, and then to decide on the price. The church pays them in coupons, according to their work. With these coupons, the parents buy the toys of their choice for their children. The day of the toy sale comes. Some church folk and some from the slum stand side by side as sale persons. There is never such natural closeness and fun between church people and the slum community. So the children have their toys, and the parents the dignity of giving. And the church has a trusting and equal relationship with the people in the slum. Everybody has fun.

This has come about because the people in the congregation remember what it is like to be parent and poor. The methodology and the spirituality of solidarity.

Let Christians therefore engage in the Isaiah Agenda and issue invitations to worship and discipleship with a sense of shared woundedness with one another and with the rest of the world. The refugee in our village is no longer someone alien who threatens our jobs and our way of life. He or she is now someone like us — a person striving to build a home and a decent life for his or her loved ones. And the secular men and women of our neighbourhood are no longer mere hedonists out for a quick fix. They are also God-seekers who have, up to now, found only the false god of Mammon. And we understand them because we too have come through this way.

With this attitude of shared woundedness, a parish stands a good chance of becoming a community and spiritual home. Christians need no longer put on masks. We can let brothers and sisters share our lives. We no longer feel ashamed of letting people know that we have needs, that we have wounds on our bodies and on our souls. And we need others to heal us and to walk with us as we lead the Christian life. In case this sounds like a pathetic clinging together of weak persons in order to escape from the world, I must hasten to say it is not so. While we do not hide the fact that we are weak, we share in order to become strong. It is a witness to our secular society, where it is difficult for people to admit their weakness to one another. Even within the family, fathers and mothers, wives and husbands, sons and daughters seldom share their weakness with one another. We communicate to others that we have no need of them. But we do. Everybody does. And we hurt. If Christians can break out of this structure of alienation, the seed is sown for our encounters with the world to be deeply meaningful.

Let me share a personal testimony. I have a twenty-year-old son. He has developed into a very independent person, capable of looking after himself with his studies, and with his friends. We are happy about that. A few years ago, my wife and I sensed that a distance had developed between us and him. At one point, he did not talk much with us. And he became overtly critical of the church. We accepted that as part of growing up. But we were still disturbed. We tried various ways to give ourselves more time together. Nothing worked. Finally, we hit on the idea of intercessory prayer at our evening meal. Instead of reciting a fifteen-second grace, we would spend one to two minutes interceding for each other — our health, our anxieties, exams, friends and relatives. We also prayed for the world, for South Africa, for the Philippines. Our relationship with our son changed. We all changed. A year ago, he was baptized.

I believe the key is solidarity. As we intercede, we show each other that we have needs. That contrary to appearances, we are not all strength and steel. In prayer, we open up to each other. Now, these short minutes of intercessory prayer around the dinner table have become a most treasured time for our family.

4. Giving an Account of Our Hope

Many churches in the ecumenical movement are not unfamiliar with the Isaiah Agenda. They have been serving and advocating the cause of the powerless and the oppressed for years. But many of them have not been able to move on to the invitation to worship and discipleship. There are many reasons for this, some worthy, some not so worthy. Probably the most common fear on the part of the Christians involved, and not an unreasonable one in theory, is that an act of invitation may endanger the partnership forged in the struggle for the Isaiah Agenda. Christians fear that our partners might misunderstand us and misread our motive.

Much of what we have said in the preceding pages has addressed this issue. Our emphasis that we engage in the Isaiah Agenda, not so much to solve the world's social and economic problems as to show forth the character of God. Our stress on the concept of partnership, which puts the Christian and others on an equal footing, thus nourishing openness and trust.

At this point, the apostle Peter's evangelism advice to the church adds a most helpful note. Peter urges his fellow believers "to be prepared always to give an account of the hope that is in us" (1 Pet. 3:15).

Two ideas stand out.

That we are to give an account of our hope to others presupposes that Christians are accountable to the world. What does this mean? It is without question that Christians are accountable to God who creates and nourishes, saves and guides us, and before whom we will stand in judgment some day. But accountability to the world? Why?

This is where evangelism comes in. Being accountable means being answerable. We are to be answerable to the world for our belief and our actions. We have the obligation to explain to people what we believe and what we do not believe, why we act in a certain way and not in other ways. Christians are not obliged to do what others tell us but we are under obligation to explain our convictions and actions. By so doing, we affirm our Christian identity and at the same time strengthen our ties with others outside the church.

Secondly, Peter suggests to us that the account Christians are to give is the account of our hope. It is not to be an account of our past and present achievement, personal or corporate. It is to be an account of what we dearly wish to be and become. The cutting edge of Christian testimony is not the perfection of our moral conduct, nor the success of our individual and corporate living. In our testimony, according to Peter, what will be inviting to others is our hope — that which is yet to be, that which we long to see happen, that which we strive to become.

This must be a most encouraging thought to those of us who are only too aware of our own shortcomings and who nevertheless wish to see others accept the Christian message and become disciples of Christ. What is required of us in evangelism is simply our hope and our determination to press on towards that hope. Our struggle towards God and towards what God wants to see happen in this world invites others to identification with us.

Let me go further. I think Christians giving an account of our hope includes giving an account of our limitations, weaknesses, fears and even failures. These too can be evangelizing. If we accept that we need to explain ourselves to the world, and that our relationship with others is one of partnership, there is no need to try to impress people and to pretend to be more than what we are. We come before the world as we are, human, broken and fearful, like everyone else, but always pressing on and always living in hope.

I recall the testimony of a friend who is a lay evangelist in south India, in an impoverished parish next to a huge slum. For years, she worked among the poor, preaching and serving, refusing offers of greener pastures.

But not many showed any clear inclinations towards the Christian way. One night, during a meeting with a group of girls who had fled their homes because of their fear of being sold into prostitution, she burst out in anger. Frustrated by the slave-like mentality of the girls who, given the terrible sufferings they had been subjected to, ought to know better, she found herself shouting at them: "The one thing that will liberate you from your bondage — the gospel, to it you have shown no response. What can I say?" She threw up her hands. The room was silent. Then a girl timidly put up her hand and said: "You have been so patient and so good to us we thought we could never hope to be like you. We can never be good enough to be Christian." My friend was shocked. But that evening proved to be a turning point in her ministry, and in the lives of many of those girls.

There is also the story of a congregation in a rather depressed area in a New Zealand town. The denomination to which the congregation belongs is known for its commitment to the cause of indigenous peoples. The congregation tried to live out the commitment, with mixed results. Its financial and human resources were limited. The congregation, while generally supportive of the denomination's direction, often did not have the same mind on specific issues. On one occasion, a group of unemployed youth made a demand on the congregation for financial help and office space. They made a strong case. And they made it in a strong manner, too strong for some of the church's lay leaders. The congregation was divided. It could not give a definitive response to the group. Suspicion grew. Confrontational tactics were introduced. Stakes were raised. At some point it became clear that even if the congregation were able to come to one mind, it would not have the resources to meet the increasing demands made on its limited resources.

The answer was found in Peter's statement about giving an account of our hope. The congregational leadership, divided on this particular issue, decided to try out Peter's advice. They frankly admitted to the group of unemployed youth their inability to come to a common response to their request. They welcomed the group to attend their next debate and to participate in it if they wished. The leadership confessed that the division was not exactly reflecting well on the church, but at the moment, that was the way it was. They felt the need to give a full account of their feelings and conflicts to this group of unemployed youth.

The invitation was totally out of the normal experience of both the church and the young people. Church members had never debated anything among themselves in the presence of non-members, and especially on a subject which would affect the latter directly. And these young people had seldom attended church, and certainly never a debate among Christians.

The church hall was packed. The two sides were fully represented. The group of unemployed youth was very loudly there with their posters. Many feared physical confrontation. But the three-hour meeting went well. It turned out to be a three-way conversation. It was frank. The displeasure of some Christians over the blunt language and arrogant behaviour of the young group, for example, was fully aired. It was honest. The needs of the poor and the young who had very little chance in life was told in first-person narratives. It was blunt, but Christian. The liberality of God and the limitations of Christians were expressed in painful reflections.

The congregation, warts and all, was giving an account of its hope and, if I may add, of its struggles and weaknesses, to this group of unemployed youth. The young people began to understand. Nobody had ever bothered to respond to them with accountability, as this congregation was doing. Nobody had ever given these trouble-makers so much time, serious attention, fairness and respect.

Thus began a process of negotiation which, in theological terms, was indeed a process of reconciliation. A solution was found. A small amount of money was set aside. Conditions were drawn up and agreed upon. It was a transaction between equals. More, it came out of a relationship of mutual accountability. The group had its office in a little room inside the church. Two years later, it became the youth fellowship of the church and the most dynamic outreach ministry in the area.

Giving an account of our hope is both an expression of our solidarity with our neighbours, and an invitation to them to examine for themselves the Christian faith.

5. Church — the People of God

How does a local congregation begin to engage in this ecumenical strategy ? What is the first step ?

The first step is theological in nature and it has immediate practical implications.

The local congregation should understand with absolute clarity that a church is primarily the people of God. The church is not a building, nor is it the clergy or the parish organization. It is the people who confess Jesus Christ, and who, the lay people and the ordained, gather regularly for worship. The church is the people of God.

It follows then that the work of the church is the work of the Christian people, and that the witness of the church is the witness of its members. Church involvement in the Isaiah Agenda means primarily the involvement of its members — from where they are : in their homes, in their village or neighbourhood, in the market place, in schools, community associations, trade unions, cooperatives, chambers of commerce, political parties, in short through their whole life and all their activities. The involvement could take the form of personal acts of kindness and of mercy. It could be organized through corporate efforts to relieve pain and suffering. Or it could be social and political action in order to deal with structural issues. But whatever the action, as long as it contributes to the Isaiah Agenda in some way, it contributes to the church's witness. It makes God better known.

A frail old church member spending time to nurse a severely undernourished child back to health. Mothers and grandmothers standing on picket lines on behalf of their disappeared children or their exploited miner husbands. Professional men and women working to safeguard the health of the community and the environment. Each and every such action carried out by Christian people constitutes the work and witness of the church. The church is the people of God.

A local congregation in southern Germany decided to follow the logic of this conviction. It planned its annual report in a different way. Instead of the traditional report which describes mainly the work done by the clergy and church officials — the number of baptisms, confirmations, deaths and marriages, and the work of various parish committees — it wanted a report consisting primarily of stories about the life and witness of its members in the community. Once the decision was made early in the year, the church came to realize almost immediately that through its members, the church had extensive and some very close contacts with almost every sector of the community. The church also quickly acquired the happy knowledge that because of the life and witness of Christian people where they were, the congregation did not need a big mission and evangelism budget, nor a great deal of organized activities and events in order to reach out to the community. At the end of the year, the annual report appeared. It carried stories of its members, some individually, others in groups that had been gathering in homes. Some could be considered success stories. Some did not show much by way of tangible results. But, following the Isaiah Agenda, they all told of how the lives of Christian men and women intersected with those of the children, the old folk and the working men and women in the community. Never before had the congregation felt so much unity and realized the scope and extent of missionary possibilities available to it.

It became apparent that every person in the congregation had gifts for witness.

Several children reported of their classmates in the neighbourhood school coming with them to Sunday school. Their parents were not church-goers and tended to stay in bed late on Sunday mornings. The children were glad to have something to do. One told of a Muslim family. The little boy there was eager to come. This posed some problems. His Christian friend didn't know what to do. He told his parents and they consulted the pastor. Together they decided that the best way was for the

Christian parents to pay a visit to their Muslim neighbours and talk things over. They were graciously received in the Muslim home. To their surprise, the response was enthusiastic. The Muslim couple were happy over Christian friendship and the acceptance of their son. They gave their blessing to their son joining his friends in Sunday school. The two families got to know each other. The pastor would also drop in occasionally just to keep the Muslim couple informed of what their son had been learning in class.

A group of old people on pension discovered that the time they had was God's greatest gift to them at this stage of their lives. Few others had such a privilege. They shared their experience of using this gift for the Isaiah Agenda.

Even suffering and tragedy can become a gift for witness.

A middle-aged business executive who was an alcoholic at one time realized that his experience could point others to God. He wrote in his part of the congregation's annual report how he shared the story of his struggle with his business colleagues.

A sexually-abused woman overcame her trauma through counselling and has begun, however tentatively, to be a source of support to others. The congregation affirmed her and encouraged her with a commitment to support any training she might find useful for the purpose.

There is need of course for the congregation to act corporately on some aspects of the Isaiah Agenda. But the strategy's emphasis is on Christian involvement as persons, families and small groups in the course of daily living, rather than on organized activities led by church authorities and financed by the congregation's treasury. This emphasis however is not to be understood solely in terms of private acts. The theology of the church as the people of God would not permit that. Christians act not as individuals but as members of the body of Christ in the very fabric of the world, utilizing the gifts of the Spirit for the sake of witness.

Once it is recognized that the witness of the congregation takes place outside the four walls of its buildings and is carried out mainly by the laity in their homes, their neighbourhood, and the market place, the role of the clergy and the elders becomes clear. Their role is to enable the laity to do a better job. This means leaders of the congregation pray for their members, and intercede for them. Not just the ones who are sick, or in need, but for all as frontline witnesses of Jesus Christ.

It also means a ministry of encouragement and of equipping: for instance, the pastor saying a kind word at the right moment, sharing a useful idea, paying a home visit, helping to form a support group, locating expert help to bear on an issue of concern, highlighting an act for the encouragement of all, preaching to teach, to empower and to honour. This presupposes a leader who listens, who bears the needs of his or her people in mind, and who is constantly on the look-out for ways to stimulate and to support.

A pastor of a congregation of mainly middle-class professionals told me that the best thing he has done by way of encouraging and equipping his people is to send to various members appropriate magazine articles which would — or should — interest them. Apparently a number of magazines and journals land on his desk. He would send an article on bio-ethics, for instance, to the health professionals in his church. He would send a series on home care of the elderly to both young adults and old folk.

There are thousands of practical ways pastors can encourage and empower their people. But the most important task is theological in nature. It is to communicate to the Christian people that what they care about at home, in the village or neighbourhood, and in the market place is also God's concern. What is considered to be primarily personal or secular is also the church's concern, and is therefore a fit subject to be brought to the attention of the congregation, and a proper item for corporate intercession and caring. When members of a congregation begin to bring their concerns and their cares to the church, they break down the artificial division between the profane and the sacred, the personal and the corporate. They become a genuine community.

This process of community-building could happen in small groups meeting at homes. But the most important time and place where this should happen is worship. At worship members of the congregation gather and bring with them their attempts to witness during the week. There their seemingly isolated, feeble, routine or secular endeavours are seen and affirmed as the endeavours of the church, and offered to God. In the process, confession is made, sins forgiven, commitment renewed, praises sung, joy experienced, and strength restored.

End Note

The three-element strategy described in this booklet is built on the evangelistic experiences of many churches in different parts of the world. The attitudes, spirituality and methodology required of this strategy, and themselves nourished by the strategy, explain much contemporary mission engagement.

I hope that by bringing them together, we would have a mirror before us. We would be able to see what our strengths and weaknesses are. Perhaps we could then become more deliberate, more consistent, and more effective.

Almost all Christian churches engage in some form of Isaiah Agenda action. Let us also articulate clearly to the world that the God we worship is a God who doesn't want to see children die, who wants old people to live in dignity and working men and women get a fair return for their labour. The world will understand this. Some will respond to our invitation to worship and discipleship. Christians in a local congregation can do this together. So can the churches in a village, a town, a city, a nation, on the face of the whole earth. The Isaiah Agenda does not recognize human boundaries.

I dream of a global, common Christian witness around the Isaiah Agenda, beginning with its first conviction that children do not die. I dream of churches worldwide, beginning with local congregations, mobilizing all their pastoral, intellectual, cultural, social, political and financial resources, in partnership with each other and all people of good will. Whoever and whatever works to reduce the number of children dying is friend and ally. Whoever and whatever causes children to die is enemy and foe.

We will have the serious attention of our neighbours and of the world.

As I put the final touches to this little manuscript, I recalled a letter a colleague of mine wrote some time back. He told me: "Many years ago when my friend's five-year old child died of congenital heart failure, I realized in a profound way how fragile and yet how strong life is. I came face to face with the central power of God's mysterious presence and action in the world and in us. It is not by works that we are saved."

Amen. So let us move and follow our God who did not send his Son into the world to condemn the world but to save the world through him. And rejoice!